TIME'S TRAVERSE

BY THE SAME AUTHOR

poetry
Retrospective
Ayrshire recessional
Climber's calendar

language
Good punctuation guide
Grammar guide
Idioms: Their meanings and origins
Scottish names

for children
Edinburgh: A capital story (with Frances Jarvie)
Scottish castles
The clans
Scotland's Vikings (with Frances Jarvie)

as editor
The wild ride and other Scottish stories
The genius and other Irish stories
Scottish short stories
A friend of humanity: Stories of George Friel
Scottish folk and fairy tales
Irish folk and fairy tales
Great golf stories
The Scottish reciter
A nest of singing birds
Writing from Scotland
Crème de la crème (with Cameron Wyllie)

Gordon Jarvie
TIME'S TRAVERSE
POEMS 1991–2001

EDINBURGH 2002

Published 2002
by Harpercroft Books
81 Comiston Drive
Edinburgh
EH10 5QT
Scotland

© Gordon Jarvie 2002

The right of Gordon Jarvie
to be identified as the author
of this work has been asserted
by him in accordance with
the Copyright, Designs and
Patents Act 1988

Book design by Mark Blackadder
Printed and bound in Scotland
by Miller Print, Glasgow

ISBN 0 95335302 8

CONTENTS

I

AYRSHIRE RECESSIONAL AND OTHER POETRY

Ayrshire recessional
    Compass bearings: Troon / 3
    The mighty fallen / 4
    Larger than life / 5
    Barnweil Hill, by Craigie / 6
    Swan Lake, by Culzean / 7
    Home / 8
    Dundonald Hill / 9

Ozymandias in Airdrie / 11
Grandma / 12
At first sight / 13
The fairy thorn tree / 14
One night in Dublin / 17
Two sides of a coin / 20
Redcurrants / 21
Bonfire / 22
Flora / 24
Reflection / 25
Born loser / 26
Before it all begins again / 27
Tadpoles / 28
Seasonal / 29
Loss / 30
But what's it *for*? / 31
The staying power of plants / 32
Pterodactyl / 34
Egypt / 36
On first looking into the Pacific Ocean / 38
The beach at Accra / 39

The editor salutes Janet Ogbo / 40
Nigerian flashback / 42
Roger / 44
Kiss / 45
Scots accent / 46
Nationality / 47
Colleague: A sketch / 48
In Brittany / 50
The day we saw the conger / 56
Smithy Cottage, Lugton / 59
How do I write a poem? / 63

II
CLIMBER'S CALENDAR

Skye nocturne / 69
Slioch / 70
Lochearnhead / 71
Into Atholl / 72
Meall Ghaordie / 74
East of Glenshee / 75
Looking west / 77
Meall nan Tarmachan / 78
The Ben / 79
Finally, the Mamores / 81
Meall Chuaich / 82
Beinn Achaladair / 83
Inaccessible Pinnacle / 84
Stuc a' Chroin / 85
Ladhar Bheinn / 86
Ben Chonzie, or Ben-y-Hone / 87

III
PORTFOLIO THREE

Time's traverse / 91
Barber-shop blues / 92
Birthday largesse / 93
Medal / 94
Brass figure / 96
Kitchen clock / 98
School reunion / 99
To my son, Andrew / 101
Sonnet for my wife / 103
Farewell to Saint-Malo / 103
La Baudunais / 104
By the river at Langon / 105
Birdwatching / 106
Suburban foxes / 107
In the name / 109
Diagnosis / 110
If . . . / 111
The Big Shepherd of Etive / 112
Walking the Monadhliath / 112
You and me / 114
Tinseltown, USA / 116
Sic transit / 116
One liners: A punnet / 117

Notes / 118
Acknowledgements / 120

I
AYRSHIRE RECESSIONAL AND OTHER POETRY

AYRSHIRE RECESSIONAL

Compass bearings: Troon

I watch the red disk of a languorous
sun's slow lapse below a western sea
off the far end of Academy Street.
Rightward the sleeping bulk of Arran.

Stars dot a darkening sky to south
above the slighter mass of Merrick,
a toenail moon etching itself from nowhere.
Orion the hunter strides out, sharp and clear.

East by Dundonald Hill a fuzzier view,
the blinds of dusk already well drawn down.
But my mind's eye picks out a court's musicians
rehearse their notes and play at Harpercroft.

North is the shortest view from where I stand,
but once again the mind's eye pictures it –
ducks fly firthward over a silent strand
and a white dune fades into a sloe-black night.

How many ocean tides have lapped and ebbed,
how many far-off flaming suns have set
upon this scene?

The mighty fallen

   Once,
she took us with her
everywhere. Now
it takes two of us
to take her anywhere.

   Then,
everything achieved at speed,
as if dear life depended on it.
Half-dragging our wee arms
from their poor sockets,
fleeing with us up the station brae
through slanting stinging rain,
shackled to her wake –
the only way for her to catch a train
was by the skin of her teeth,
shouting at startled railwaymen
to 'Hold that train!'

We inch along so slowly now,
one dragging foot at a time,
getting there, more or less,
pulling along with stick or zimmer frame.
But it is wonderful to see her smile
and watch her travel hopefully
in her inimitable and indomitable style,
even if subsided in that chair,
that nest of rugs and cushions.

She used to be so strict with us,
applying well aimed slap or noisy scold.
Now in turn we have to be so firm with her,
and wrap her up against encircling cold
if we are going to take her anywhere.

Larger than life

The hard bit
is watching loved ones
diminished
who were once
so much larger than life;

whose lives once shone
(we like to think)
to enlighten our darkness
themselves flickering
and dimming towards their dusk.

For then we know
it's our turn
to raise our game
and throw our afternoon light
into their shadows –

trying to bring them
out of their soul's dark night.
The big fear then is this: Will
our batteries be strong enough
to see them through?

Barnweil Hill, by Craigie

Then: 1296

Distant defiance of blue Arran hill,
white mirror slash of water in the sun,
an airy sky goes whistling by,
the Barns o Ayr burn weel, quo I,
where Braveheart went in for the kill.

There fell the English governor of Ayr
with his lippy bumptious myrmidons.
The patriot Wallace dished out justice there
and even the town's friar deaf to their orisons –
for hadn't they just tricked and slaughtered Scotia's sons?

Now: 1996

Today four of us sit in the car
by a whitewashed hilltop farm
and a tree-girt sandstone monument:
two old ladies enjoy the summer view,
a boy itches to explore it all, and I.
A lazy dog in the farmyard barks,
the blue sky fills with the singing of larks,
life tiptoes by.

A notice regrets the Wallace Tower is shut,
but the farmer has slung a long rope swing
from a high-branched elm nearby. So,
good as it might have been to climb that stair,
the boy from the car wastes little time to show
a better way up through the lark-filled air
to celebrate the deeds of Braveheart, the hero.

Swan Lake, by Culzean

For some reason, my walks here seem
uncannily remembered, clear as last night's dream.

So much else forgotten, somehow they
get kept and kept, and are not thrown away.

The last time: an early summer afternoon,
sunny and warm, a-buzz with bees in June.

In a distant field a flock of – surely not? – ostriches;
big and black and white, ridiculous as witches.

You in the wheelchair urged me along,
unperturbed by muddy paths or approaching swan.

The time before, we walked. You took frequent seats and an arm
apiece from Andrew and me. It was thundery and warm.

Longer ago, we tried out binoculars and a red pushchair
here. That day, his big sister was the passenger.

Once with Dad here, I had a brisk and serious talk
about What I Would Do With My Life. That was a winter walk.

One teenage springtime I sat here under birch trees
with my valentine. We heard heartbeats in the breeze.

Far-away childhood picnics I can just about recall
playing the livelong day here, earliest memories of all.

Will there be further visits here, alone or with folk I cherish?
I don't know. But these snapshots neither dull nor perish.

Home

Going there to visit her on Sundays,
giving the week's account of myself
and hearing bits of hers: for years it was
our regular parent–child exchange.

Thus even yesterday
thirty-odd winters after quitting the parental nest
it was still a place
I sometimes called home.

Today it's just a little Ayrshire town
because she who I'd foolishly begun
to believe to be immortal
left us last night.

Dundonald Hill

In November we sat here
watching a wintry sunset –
blues, yellows, eerie pinks
stretching far beyond Kintyre
away and away and away.

I took some photos for you that day,
no one in them, just the view
from this, your favourite vantage point
of many a year. After your weekly shop,
you used to like to sit with Dad here
and drink in that scene, light playing
across the surface of the varying firth –
sometimes seething in a westerly gale,
sometimes becalmed . . .

It's nearly Christmas now.
This morning I sit here alone
and at my back a winter sun creeps up.
Rays feel their speculative ways
through blue-grey haze
and probe towards the sea.

Right now they are invisible but I know
that Arran's peaks are over there;
leftward is Ailsa Craig, and then
the tapering Carrick Hills
and Heads of Ayr.

And if I shut my eyes a moment
hard against the misty glare
and steady myself, I know
you too are here again,
just as we were.

Arran, from Troon

OZYMANDIAS IN AIRDRIE

Once long ago my Grandpa Beattie
took me by tram out to the country
past Airdrie, I think. We took a walk there
past a colossal building, boarded up.

Aged about eight, I asked what it was. He said
it had been the biggest blotting-paper factory
in the whole world, but closed since folk had recently
gone from using ink pens to biros overnight.

I know from the rhyme that an ink-dipped pen
was a boon and a serious blessing to men
and to blotting-paper factories, but why oh why
didn't these folk anticipate trends and diversify?

Did they watch a moving finger write
and having writ move on? Did they lack wit to see
that factories are valued not for what they make
but what they sell? Or did they see, and their hands shake?

Who knows – poor sad turkeys failing to escape
Christmas, harbingers of a post-industrial landscape.
Why did my grandpa take me for that walk?
Too late now to ask, too late for talk. This I recall:

Our sadness at lost jobs was palpable, at a village's despair
at nothing left to do. I picture still sclerosis and decay
creep over that redundant workshop, silent and bare,
where a lone and windswept hillside drops away.

GRANDMA

Veteran player of an endless street,
she seems to own the thronging crowd
we pass among and through.

Clasping some stranger's hand
she often comes away
with awesome civilities
which I can only whisper half-aloud:
'Sure, but you're looking great.
Can it be twenty years since last I saw ye?'

Aged less than half of that, I wholly fail
to grasp how she can possibly recall
so long the look of someone's face.
Do time or memory not alter them?
Are they indelible?

Yesterday I lunched with a man
I hadn't seen for twentysomething years,
and suddenly I was thinking again
about the magisterial assurance
of those greetings and perambulations,
those throwaway lines of repartee.
Grandma, would you not be proud of me
now that I too have survived this long?

Twenty years? Twenty quid?
A child and a fool imagine
they'll never be spent. Truly,
of all the things that happen to a person,
old age is the most unexpected.

AT FIRST SIGHT

A plain wooden bench up on a clifftop walk,
alone you sit there, gazing away and away
over and beyond a distant sea.

I come alongside
and you smile at me.
Nothing is said, or needs to be.

Walking that way another time I find
I'm detouring around by that windy parade
in the hope of a second sighting.

And when against the gale you do stroll into view,
I so mistrust my own two eyes that I
must pinch myself and sit down on the grass,
because my heart is seething like the elements.

This time you saunter up and sit with me.
Alone we sit and look upon a boiling sea.

THE FAIRY THORN TREE

In those more innocent times
before the latest Troubles
I hitched to country places
like Dungiven.

On arrival, driven
to the very door – 'No trouble, son' –
you are quizzed at length
about your driver. Would that
be Maguire the vet
or his brother Joe from up the Feeny road
by Knockan Bridge?
It isn't nosiness so much
as plain proof of country living
where everybody knows everybody
whatever their 'persuasion'.

On the Saturday afternoon,
a sunny windy day,
the rector takes us shooting, his son and I.
To my surprise, the man turns out
a dead-eye shot, and him a clergyman.
He bags as many snipe in half an hour
as I'd caught mackerel a month before
a mile out of Troon harbour with my dad.

Afterwards, striding across a blustery moor
behind a house called Pellipar he takes great pride
in showing me an ancient skeagh-bush –
a squat and stunted little blackthorn tree
stuck in a shallow hollow

at the dead centre of nowhere,
but so decked out with bits of rag and cloth
that it appears a strange lost Christmas thing
beached on a summer strand.

Some of its rags are leprous and snot-green,
so it is not a thing of mystery
or beauty – rather just a scabby emblem
to a folk superstition
that still flourishes hereabouts
when nobody is looking.

Sunday turns out a busy day
for a country rector, even one
semi-retired 'from active combat'.
My host – surely in great demand? –
appears to spend his day driving about
to this or that outpost of his faith
for communion or evensong
or some other celebration.
I wonder idly if any of the churches
where he performs
might have decked themselves out
as fervently and tastelessly
as that little fairy thorn tree.

Coda

Twentysomething years on
from that weekend in another country –
or was it in another world? –
I sit in the morning bustle of a street cafe

somewhere off London's Piccadilly
sipping cappuccino while I make
urgent, last-minute preparations
for a strategic business meeting
of such paramount importance
that I've long forgotten what it was about.

Then across that cafe's hum and two decades
I hear a voice I know – English vowels
in a swirl of Irish mist, and I recognise
the speech of my one-time school friend,
the Ulster rector's son. Hailing him, I say,
'You're a long way from the fairy thorn tree.'

The startled head swings round to face me
with quickly dawning grin. 'Och aye,'
he mimicks in his best stage Scots,
'It has to be, it cannae be ither
than my auld freend Rabbie Burns,
the Ayrshire plooman.' We shake hands . . .

ONE NIGHT IN DUBLIN

A cold and wintry snap,
a light frosting of snow
dusts the dozing town
under a prescient yellow moon.

On such evenings –
even on Fridays –
the warmth of the Reading Room
is almost an attraction
and I get stuck in
to my *Pilgrim's Progress*.

Tonight a muffled restlessness
disturbs the studious calm.
Is it me, hankering for a wild weekend,
or is there something else?

Ten o'clock. A bell rings, so soon.
A tide of students
ebbs from a round room,
returns borrowed books
and seeps out into the white crispness
of Front Square.

I pause and light a cigarette.
A friend asks, through the gloom,
Did you hear? Hear what? I ask,
recalling the uneasy ripples
across the Reading Room
and the knelling bell. A doom?

We talk, and then go separate ways.
I, in a blank daze
enter a pub to watch it all
on a merciless blue screen
high on a bar-room wall.

Old Bartkus buys me a beer.
I sip at it, trying to take this story in.

From Vanity Fair,
beyond Doubting Castle
and across the River of Death,
with all his marks and scars
Mr President has today passed over.
Today the trumpets sounded for him
upon the other side.

Looking around this room
I read one thought
on every silent face and taut
now he is gone from Camelot:
Who will fight Giant Despair for us now
and help us through this dark shadow?

Postscript, 1997

This poem happened many years ago
as I began to weigh the passing years.
It describes a spasm of my world's soul
even farther back in time. It is
a yellowing snapshot of a young man's tears.

A life's defining moments don't recede. Today
is a sunny summer morning thirty-four years on
from that far-off distress. An older man
and world wake up to learn
of another violent death.

This death of a princess is a strange demise.
A chauffeur-driven butterfly caught in a gyre
has flown inexorably at a funeral pyre
of her own creation, intoxicated
on the oxygen of her own publicity,
an accident dying to happen,
hoist on her own petard.

Another of their mother's photo opportunities,
I pity her poor children now bereft. I pity too
an older generation impelled to remember
a wintry night in November
so very long ago.

TWO SIDES OF A COIN

I remember the smiling centenarian,
rather doddery getting into his church pew,
the crumpled dark suit, the whiff of nicotine
and stale urine, the fondness for children,
the fitful flickers of an old-time disciplinarian.

She remembers a big black cloud of a dominie
who seventy years before, and more,
had personally intervened to ensure
she got six of the best for a careless slip-up
in her Gaelic-to-English translation . . .

Hearing of his death I mutter
something inane and condolatory.
But a dark shadow passes across her gaze
before she takes a deep breath, and zestfully
pronounces the world a better place without him.

REDCURRANTS

Was it the redcurrants and perhaps
the time of year: a September day,
fine, sunny, clear, but with a tang
of winter sharpnesses to come?

Such days are bright jewels in our archives,
whatever else they are.

I recall the clean taste of the fruit
and their crimson perfection under nets
as we walked round a walled garden
on a hillside behind Innerleithen.

But like a small black cloud
across the Tweed over by Traquair
I recall too some background shadow
from which we were emerging,
and which seemed to make
a bright day even brighter,
leaving us free to focus once more
on the next steps of our journey –
at last no weight on our minds,
and once again, thank God,
no sleepless nights.

        Redcurrants
remind me how good life can be.

BONFIRE

What is it that's so right about a bonfire,
drawing us moth-like to its naked flame?
Is it the standing and gazing at it,
blank, pensive, dizzy, empty –
so purposefully idle that you spin before it,
one with the spinning world?
Its sparking ember rockets bring you to.

Is it the burning up a summer's garden rubbish,
making waste places straight?
Is it that special smell
of leaf and woodsmoke
carried on clothes and hair?

An autumn nip is on the air,
thin sun hazy on turning leaves –
less yellow fruitiness
than wan reminder of summers
going their sundry ways.

Wan? Not really so.
A little blue perhaps the smoke,
but my small helpers zing with energy,
darting about with red and glowing twigs.
Their growing shadows dance around the fire.

The clocks go back tonight.
We win an hour from Father Time
as winter is declared – official.
Here is an hour in hand, and
Halloween is just a week away.
Mist, witches, broomsticks, turnip lanterns –
a special time of year.

An hour, a week, a year?
Well, Old Man Time, I watch my childish helpers,
and it's as if you give me back a lifetime
in the flash and crack of a sparking branch,
in a zonked-out smoky stare
at the fixed point
in the red heart of a fire
about thirty years ago.

FLORA

All day I sit in the meeting
and they talk and talk.
The hee-haw Oxbridge voices rise and fall.
I watch the lips move but their words fail me.
My thoughts are many miles away
where you prepare to make your lifetime's trip.

Please take things gently, please take care.
Will you be gone, will you be there
when I get home?

You played so many parts in all our lives –
friend, neighbour, parent, granny, seasoned guide.
Flora, I have so much to thank you for,
and there is nothing now that I can do
to spare you what I know
you're going through.

'I need to pack it in,' you said,
'I'm weary now. It won't go on much more.'
Hearing those words, my heart fell to the floor
although I knew how very right you were.

We sat and listened to the clock awhile.
Nothing was said, and everything.
I held your hand, and thought of all those tins
of baby food downstairs that morning,
wondering would you even manage to eat that.

'Stay with us as long as you can,' I brought
myself to say in feeblest way.
'Now who will eat the baby food?' I thought.

REFLECTION

I like to look in shop windows
sometimes. It costs nothing.
Nobody tries
to sell you stuff or hassle you
with 'How may I help you?'
or 'Something you require?'

Stroll up the street,
stop where you desire,
stand and stare – wineshops
are good sometimes,
and it can take me half an hour
to navigate a bookshop window.

You sometimes get surprises
even in shop windows: yesterday I did.
Coat collar upturned,
who was that wispy old scruff
loitering in the street behind me,
reflected in the window pane?

Turning around to see who's there,
I laugh a hollow laugh
as bitter-sweet I hear the penny drop.
Aweel, I sigh, that really is no gift
to see myself as others do,
reflected in the window of this shop.

Is that faceless old scarecrow really me?
No, it is not in me but vainly
in my children that I like to see
myself. They are still young
and beautiful.

BORN LOSER

Five words are the querulous refrain
of such a hopeless person:
'Has *any*body seen my specs?'

He leaves his gloves or hat upon the train,
'mislays' his file of research at the library,
once – most grievously – lost his wedding ring,

is known not seldom to become
strangely detached from scarf and other things;
only last week contrived to lose a wallet

and all the personal stuff therein: the plastic
cheque cards, membership IDs
and various open sesames –

the vital formal detritus
of an ongoing existence, besides an oh-
so-precious photo of his daughter as a child.

Long ago, maybe worst of all, within five minutes
of first setting foot in New York, he was 'relieved'
of a suitcase containing his very core –

a file stuffed with a decade's poems,
his twenties wiped out in the time it took
to ask directions for Stony Brook,

Long Island. Later, he was to reach his destination
still shaking. Even today I shake
at the memory of it.

BEFORE IT ALL BEGINS AGAIN

Some mornings, lying awake
and listening to the intensity
of silences before the clocks go off
and everything begins again,
it's as if I hear a taxi
waiting at the front door,
its engine running quietly.

And I lie there
thinking, 'Can it be
time's wingèd chariot?

Again? Already?'

TADPOLES

More than
a nine days' wonder,
they are a yearly miracle.

The spawn a sign
of frogs' benison,
an annual visitation.

The jerking, wriggling
black question marks
pose their eternal why.

We witness their cycle
through a hindsight of years,
a shrug of tears.

Their formlessness assumes
such precise shape, follows
such predestined sequence.

The back legs minuscule,
the disappearing tail,
the swelling 'head' –

then suddenly front legs
and – presto! – wee frogs,
entirely perfect of form.

We encourage them, of course,
if only in the pious hope
of seeing quivering blobs of spawn

again, another year; and for the joy
of saying another time,
'Guess what's appeared in the pond!'

SEASONAL

Winter day, Indiana

Through these ice-patterned window-panes I stare.
We meet, the world and I, on this cold sill.
Across my breath, out of this whitened air
I first smell blood run chill.

Winters here are grey. Even grass
when it appears is grey after the snows.
Streets, faces, sidewalks, feelings – all are grey,
and skies are heavy, leaden, and foreclosed.

Spring, in an Edinburgh park

Livid dappled greenwood scene,
buds of May bursting with urgency,
sharp, foliage fresh, and squeaky clean –
in beryl, emerald, lime, aquamarine,
a dozen verdant shades of tingling green.

Then after rain, the pungent, rutty smells,
the hint of sap and undergrowth –
of garlic crushed and spunky hint
of hawthorn, tang of campion and sloe,
the unfurling evolution of the ferns.

Here now is fullness, an effulgent whiff
to keep a 'grand parfumier' sharp of nose.
Here is a riotous rapture to sustain
Van Gogh, Cézanne, or Matisse on tiptoes
straining to make art approach this artless scene,
this greenwood's fragrant flaunting of the green.

LOSS

Emerging from the kirk
with my family
into a howling wind,
someone observed
my tear-stained cheek
and asked me
what was on my mind.

Nothing much, I replied.
I am merely lamenting
the long-lost certainties
of my childhood.

BUT WHAT'S IT *for*?

For some considerable time
she stands and looks at it.
Next she runs off a little way
and then comes back,
pursing her lips,
giving the thing
her quantity surveyor look
and frowning her quizzical appraisal,
hanging her head to one side,
then shaking it hard –
maybe in disbelief?

Next comes the tactile approach
as she rubs her hands
across the shiny silver
of its flat rippling surfaces,
then taps it,
listens awhile,
and smacks it hard.

Is that a satisfying noise
which appeals to her? Maybe.
Inspecting for some time contentedly,
she smacks it here and there.

Finally she looks at me and asks,
'What is it?' And I say,
'A sculpture.' Then the harder question,
'But what's it *for*?' (her emphasis).
And I reply, 'For looking at.'

Unsatisfied with my answer perhaps
as only a three-year-old can be,
she thumps it again, hard as she can.

THE STAYING POWER OF PLANTS

For Sally

Aged about two,
with muddy but triumphant gardener's face,
I remember the day
you didn't so much plant it
as shove it in its tiny flowerpot,
not into a prepared soil but
into your gooey mud-pie mix.

Like you it throve.
It several times outgrew its little pot,
but I could never bring myself
to throw out 'Sally's plant'. It has
no other name for me. I only know
I have repotted it four or five times
just as I did today into
more spacious quarters,
more room to grow.

Like you its roots have always
nicely filled the space provided.
Like you it now stands tall.
But though it does not flower –
does not do *any*thing but grow –
I have to grant it is
my favourite household plant.
That is because it is for me
a little evergreen offshoot
of your innocence.

Also I begin to see
that it will be here still,
long after you
have spread your wings.

Thus do I realise it's wrong of me
to underestimate the sheer longevity,
the earthbound staying power
of plants.

PTERODACTYL

For Wilma Horsbrugh

This is the tale of a pterodactyl
extinct for quadrillions of years.
    It slept frozen stiff
    at the foot of a cliff
un-noticed, or so it appears.

And then the climate got warmer,
causing the icecap to thaw,
    till the ice round it broke
    and the creature awoke,
astonished by all that it saw.

At first it remained quite immobile.
Then suddenly, after a week,
    'I'd better get moving,'
    it muttered – thus proving
pterodactyls are able to speak.

The folk of St Leonards that morning,
got a horrible frightening surprise,
    when something enormous came stumbling
    down the cragside quite audibly mumbling –
a *thing* of incredible size!

The creature tried to be friendly
so its feelings were dreadfully hurt
    when the folk ran away.
    Then they all heard it say,
'Humans treat pterodactyls like dirt.'

The poor thing, although it took umbrage,
persevered in its efforts to charm them.
    But by wagging its tail
    it created a gale –
most dramatic, and bound to alarm them.

'St Leonards folk,' mused the creature,
'Were hostile to me from the start.
    And it's only too clear
    that I'm not wanted here.
I'd be wiser, I'm sure, to depart.

'This earth I'm obliged to abandon.
To Mars I shall fly, and quite soon.
    On second thoughts not,
    for Mars is too hot.'
So it set off that night for the moon.

And space travellers now in the Nineties
on the moon have observed a new feature.
    For there frozen stiff
    in a vast lunar cliff
they've discovered a curious creature –
        a pterodactyl!

EGYPT

Everyone asked
what I thought of the pyramids.

I said,
I saw schools and classrooms,
teachers giving English from textbooks
to classfuls of eager children
slightly unsure of our presence,
too polite to come right out
and ask what we were doing there.
But they plainly wondered
had we come to inspect them?

Much welcoming: bowing and smiling,
shaking of hands, quite formal.
That is the end of the lesson,
most of the teachers say, as if
to suggest we can go now.
What happens then, I wonder –
not that I'm much good at being
a fly on the wall of another culture.
Spectator sports
were never my strongest card.

Traffic-clogged streets
and trips to the ministry. Armed outriders
and wailing escorts and then
the official car. That was
the minister, someone whispers.
Such style. But that is it –
that's as near as we get. Ministers are

too high-powered and armour-plated
for the likes of us. So we sit
with the English Counsellor
for more smiles and words of welcome;
and little cups of karkaday to sip –
a red drink, sweet and refreshing,
made from dried flowers of hibiscus.

The draft proposal is sketched
for the Counsellor's approval. We wait to see;
and then the nod, the smile, the invitation
to come back tomorrow, and discuss
matters in more depth. Good – this is success,
this is what we came for.

      Outside the town,
the sphinx smiles on into another sunset,
the wonders of an ancient world unvisited yet.

And the pyramids? I don't know,
I said. I haven't seen them yet.

ON FIRST LOOKING INTO THE PACIFIC OCEAN

That day I stared at Pacific's wide expanse,
silent, from a wee hill in Valparaiso
scanning the horizon of the Spanish Main
for realms of gold, for goodly states and kingdoms.
It looked to me like any other hazy glimpse of sea
viewed from a certain distance: the English Channel, say,
seen from the Kemptown racecourse, or maybe
the Firth of Forth from somewhere up behind Dunbar
where Cromwell wrought his havoc once.

Later, leaving Chile on an eighteen-hour flight
from Santiago, is ample time to tell myself
that official British export missions, replete
with formal receptions at the embassy –
First Commercial Attaché holding court here
(posing under shimmering cut-glass chandelier),
Under-Secretary of something-or-other glittering there
(polished foot resting on gilt-paint Empire chair) –
are perhaps not the ideal location in which
to be caught nodding over Chapman's Homer.

THE BEACH AT ACCRA

Blaze of steel-grey sea, shimmering splash of sand,
warm breeze blowing from sea to land.
A bunch of holy rollers, drenched in pious ecstasy,
throw themselves about the blistering strand,
moaning, lowing, bellowing deliriously,
looking as if they might do themselves
some less-than-godly injury.

Slow fisherfolk sort massive nets, and go about
livelihoods with careful, biblical consideration.
Visiting folk, from hotels or airlines, sit in shade
sipping atmosphere, club cocktails, lazy syncopation
to strains of Ebenezer Obay and his Dark City Sisters.
Myself, and a scatter of intrepid souls, heave out
in a massive surf, shrieking
at the white noonday enormity of it all.

Moored offshore two bluish outlines, cargo boats,
brought out the early morning crowds
and queues of ever-hopeful shoppers.
The shops are out of oil and soap
and I don't know what. What's the hope
for a place where oil-palm grows wild, and they can't
supply their own market needs?

That evening at the hotel, declining wine I spread
imported Dutch butter on my bread, and learn
it's all a false alarm. The boats are empty –
a mirage. No stocking up in town today.

THE EDITOR SALUTES JANET OGBO

For Ron Heapy

I
Bright as a button, big-eyed,
keen as mustard, slate in hand,
you walk three miles in the cool
of the morning to your bush school.
Pondering to ingest a day's wisdom,
you then walk back the same three miles
in the torpor of a Takoradi afternoon in Ghana.

Braided hair teased out by loving hands,
neat in blue cotton dress and sandals,
you carry on your head your case of books
as if it were the crown jewels of Asante
or an unexploded bomb-cluster of western learning.

II
For nigh on thirty years, hacking a way
through the jungle of a thousand texts
and endless books, I picture you
in a clear mind's eye. Always the question is
the same: 'What would Janet Ogbo make of this?'

The usual answer – 'Not a lot!' – means stripping
the text back to basics, simplifying it perhaps,
clarifying messages, cutting out fancy bits,
pruning digressions within digressions,
paring away tricks, amplifying the drift
where brambling verbiage hides the textual path –
until such time as one and all can say,
'*Now* is the meaning plain!'

III

Dear Janet, would you be amused to know
that you are still – for me – as you first started out,
a bonny twelve-year-old schoolgirl? My mind
rejects the notion that your own children
have been through school, and now are busy
raising babies of *their* own. Like an old photo,
my memory keeps you as you always were for me.

How are you coping, Janet Ogbo, after all these years?
Across two continents and three decades I salute you.

NIGERIAN FLASHBACK

We cross the bridge into Onitsha,
my Yoruba friend and I.
He fearful of his reception,
a war only just resolved;
I – his cover – also watchful,
my first trip to former Biafra.
Will anyone want to see us?
Will they be hostile or friendly?
Are we too soon to do business?

One end of the bridge still down,
a pontoon contraption there. The road
from the Niger up the long hill to town
showing plenty of signs of action –
craters, buildings pocked with gunshot,
some baldy looking palm trees
lying at palm-wine drunken angles . . .
We wonder how it has been,
and who has survived.

First port of call the old CMS bookshop
to seek out Mr Nwankwo.
It's just as it was, says my Yoruba friend.
Look at their wonderful textbooks.
Where did all this come from?
Who paid for all this, he wonders
aloud, as I follow him through
the darkened cool of the warehouse.

Oh greetings Olaiya, comes the call
from the green depths of the building.
Then they seem to fall on each other:
much hugging and patting of backs,
loud rolls of deep laughter, they
walk about holding hands,
perhaps afraid to lose touch again
with each other.

Congratulations, man, you survived,
is the gist of the conversation.

Coda

Later, I learned what had happened,
after the death of my Yoruba friend,
he and I that had travelled in Igboland
and been made welcome and feted
in erstwhile enemy territory.

One day, among his own people,
for so-called political reasons,
he was doused in petrol and set alight
in front of his wife and children.
Pray for that outraged body and his soul's repose.

He had backed the losing side
in an irascible election campaign,
forgetting man's fathomless savagery.
So a volatile mob of his townsmen
went to his house and did that to him.

ROGER

Today I saw Roger,
but not my Roger. It shook me
to see that look on him, not his.
I knew he'd been unwell, but not
until I saw him did I realise
how many rounds he'd gone
with the grim reaper,
and that he wasn't
looking forward to another bout.

A day at a time, he said,
which is fair comment.
I nodded. We shook hands
with some emotion, and I knew
that he was holding on.

Then we helped him into his taxi
and my old friend was gone.

KISS

From that white sepulchre his bed
he held a gaunt cheek up,
but it was twenty years
since I had kissed him last.
Thus – when it mattered much – I failed
to pick his plaintive signal up.

With gestured smile, handclasp, and wave,
I left the bed numb and unthinking. But
driving home I understood, heart sinking,
the meaning of that grave gesture,
and realised how ultimately
I had betrayed him.

These moments cannot be rehearsed,
they are disastrous and unbearable.
There is no second shot at them.

SCOTS ACCENT

After the talk, in some
unlikely place like Wimbledon,
a lady from the audience came to bray:
'I lurved your accent. I could've
listened to it all day.'

My response was less impertinent
than quizzically meant. I said:
'Never mind how I speak, my deah.
Did you by any chance get to heah
what I was trying to say?'

NATIONALITY

'Nationality?' asks
the uniformed customs man
from behind
his glass screen.

'British,' I mouth
into the bullet-proof fishtank.

Fingering my passport as if
it is a thing distasteful,
unclean, even infectious,
he turns to a uniformed
colleague and hisses at him,
'Engleesh.'

      'No, no,' I enunciate
back at him. 'Scottish.'

'Oh, move along,' he growls
with dark Levantine frown,
drawing from some deep well
of despotic irritation.
'Can't you see
that we're busy?'

COLLEAGUE: A SKETCH

Warrior matriarch, something between
Ma Slessor and old Boudicca the queen,
she revels in her woman's burdens
and attends her flagging myrmidons.

Are they still wet behind the ears,
this brood of hers? She steers
them cheeping through the undergrowth,
away from ambush
by some lurking quango
fearful for its poxy territory.

In the background —
strictly off the record, of course,
gnats, gadflies, sniping mandarins
and clouds of civil servants buzz about
with gaping unconvincing grins,
covering their flanks,
disclaiming responsibility
if anything goes wrong,
shuffling their papers.
Lethally inscrutable.

Through it all
she exhorts with winning smile
from faltering foot soldiers
one extra mile.

Face soft with the afterglow
of Christmas, she informed
me how she'd become a grandmother
again. I saw the warrior transformed,

domestic matriarch to a younger brood,
offering piggy-backs under a tinsel tree,
hunkered down behind a sofa
for hide-and-seek.

Will her babies recall these festal scenes
when they are gangling
through their gawky teens?
They may remember the enthusiast
who shared high days and holidays with them,
the hundred percenter, the person
who was not mealy-mouthed,
was not a half-measures person,
someone who filled a room.

But will they ever know
hers was the face
that ran a Scottish Office roadshow
and launched a thousand project writers?

And I? Pianissimo, I
am a sort of second clarinet
seconded to the vast symphony orchestra
where she is resident conductor. I
go to her for help with my score,
which mercifully she knows,
and gives.

IN BRITTANY

10 July

Today we lie abed listening to country noises.
A rooster crows, quite loud, on nearby hill.
Another answers further off –
and then another one, just audible.
A distant dog barks. Someone is sawing wood
a mile or so away.
Rising at noon, I plant my mimosa tree,
all three trembling feet of her,
in the shade of our hazel clump and of the little oak.
At lunch we open a bottle of Cramoisay
to handsel this addition to our landscape.

Today is the first day of our holiday,
and it is hot.

13 July

Where to go?
In all the villages
a late-night *bal musette* and firework show.
slow, slow, quick-quick slow.

By Langon church a wired-up, microphoned chanteuse
is belting out the numbers while the booze
flows freely from a huckster's makeshift stall
under a warm and inky sky – *la belle étoile*.
Today – *la veille du quatorze juillet*.

We drive on through the sticky, moth-live dark
to Beslé by the river and the park.
Here too the kids are all up late to see
the fireworks and festivity.

At midnight to loud gasps along the quay
we get what we have all stayed up to see –
the flares, the flashes and the shooting stars,
the noisy firecracks and the jollity.

A smoky, sulphurous, enchanting whiff
pervades the winking fairylights.

19 July

In shimmering heat
today they cut the yellow wheat.
The shards of dusty chaff and gritty stoor
fly through the open windows and the door
and now lie thick and deep
upon our unswept kitchen floor.

25 July

Last night we watched a lightning storm
dance over and light up our flashing skies.
For half an hour we stood and gawped
at entertainment not available on Sky TV
and were reminded of our littleness.

In a strange half-dark it started
away to the south, like heavy breathing
far off in front of the house
and over the maize fields. A sudden coolness,
distant drums of thunder, searing flashes
and zigzag lights – pinks, yellows, greens,
quiet at first, then louder, closer, *here*,
as gusts of rain began to shake the trees
with plopping spots of wet. And then,
better than Beethoven,
the blatter and crashing overhead.

We watched, then hugged each other for a while,
as our ancestors would have done
at such a scary thing. Then a farewell sigh,
and just as suddenly as it came, it passed
away to the north behind the house,
and we ran through to watch it disappear
rumbling over the valley ridge of our world.

Andrew did a raindance then, for relief,
on the dark road. We heard only
the downpipes from our roof gargoyling water.
Our waterbarrels, empty, dry, hot this afternoon,
now overflowing. And overhead –
bats in a cooler, moonlit sky. And everywhere
the sweet, slaked smell of quenching earth
and of deep-drinking hazel trees.

28 July

Aren't the acorns here voluptuous,
round and full and green –
and in July too.
Not the scrunty wee things
that pass for acorns in Scotland
in late September.

29 July

Slowly, I'm digging a ditch in front of the house,
a run-off channel for those fierce flash-floods
you get here after thunder and lightning.
Maybe it'll make some sort of patio
one day. Who knows?

The postman thinks I'm mad
to work in such a heat. *Un mercénaire,*
he calls me with a shake of the head.
Urging caution, he leaves a letter
and drives off in his yellow car.

Sweating copiously, I dig another metre
then pause for breath and beer.

30 July

We know that Paris is on holiday now.
There are hairdos in the village, and gold sandals,
and men with handbags. There were two
of them at the baker's this morning.

I caught the heavenward-glancing shrugs,
the slightest Gallic upping of an eyebrow
between two elderly locals,
which said it all.

4 August

Summer wholeness,
our valley world
now ripe to its core,
trees full and green and fruiting,
yellow fields sighing with corn,
maize stems well formed.

The world fixed and still,
the house snoozing,
I step outside to watch dusk's onset
as long blue shadows slide
into the dim husk of night
beneath a ghosting moon.

I jump. A phantom grey moth
careers with sudden bump
against my forehead,
veering into a velvet sky
and the soft silent jaw
of an approaching bat.

12 August

The megaliths scattered over the heath at Saint-Just
are white teeth in a shimmering heat.
Never exactly busy this last three thousand years,
we have them to ourselves this morning.

Today we show them to the cousins
who climb on them. They enjoy
the shaded rockface at Le Val,
conveniently replete
with piton-ringed metal spikes
to take their ropes.

Below, across the gleaming water of the lake
the streaking blue of kingfishers.

THE DAY WE SAW THE CONGER

For Jamie Mitchell, who saw it first, but not that day

Sometimes a conger eel
is longer than a man
and thicker than his upper arm.
With bulldog gargoyle head
it is a deep-sea creature
ugly and black as sin,
shiny and alligator strong,
something to haunt a child's dreams
for a year or two.

This one was all of the above and more,
and it presumed to stray
too close inshore that summer day,
lurking on a tide-wracked channel's floor
among dark jagged rocks
and swaying fronds of weed.

Moving against the ocean's flow
just once too often,
it drew attention to itself
and met its frantic fate:
a weekend snorkel fisherman's harpoon
between the staring eyes.

The seething struggle that ensued
matched two noble antagonists.
The wounded eel thrashed furiously,
trying to unskewer itself
and turn on its attacker.

Keeping the harpoon arrow
at careful arm's length,
and the whirling dervish on the end of it,
the man duly managed to surface
and resolutely drag the thing inshore.

Finally man and eel lay beached
in the shallows of the bay,
each gathering strength for the final fling,
each needing to ensure the battleground
was in *his* element: the eel's the deep sea
and the man's the land.

Tide ebbing like the sea-beast's life,
the man had the simpler strategy:
to stake it flailing to the sand
and watch it gradually strand
and fail under a bloody sun.

The sun dropped west, the tide
went back, black rocks emerged
like shark fins in the bay.
Curious children waved and called,
motioning to parents and to friends
to come and see. A small crowd gathered,
a photographer captured the moment,
a young child dropped ice cream
in the sand and began to cry.

And the fisherman? Eventually,
still in his shiny wet-suit,
with concentration and with difficulty –
for he was not young –
he tottered up the beach
dragging his still skewered catch

and dropped it, big as himself,
but dull and almost shrinking now
from life, into an old grey van
and drove away.

It had started out
as just another hot day
in a long hot summer –
a day for a steep-sloping beach
on the Cote Sauvage, for wallowing
in Atlantic waves and keeping cool.

But now, of course, it was
just another day no longer.
Now it had entered myth and was
'the day we saw the conger'.

SMITHY COTTAGE, LUGTON

*In 1850 the upland hamlet of Lugton
had four houses: a hotel, a smithy,
and two toll houses for the stage*

*plying from Glasgow to Kilmarnock.
Pell-mell then came – and went – ironworks,
railways, brickworks, and the present day.*

Today I cannot pass that old white smithy
without thinking of two spinster aunts
who lived there once.

Artists both, smart
as two pins, even their hats
were memorable.

They used to come to us
sometimes for laughter
or for supper.

I realised they were not young
that day when one of them
failed to complete

an autumn walk with us
around the reservoir.
'We're getting on,' they said.

Above all proud of their name –
my name. 'A good Scots name,
as good as anyone's,' they said.

At ten – I think – they took me
once or twice to meetings
of the Geographical Society.

We thought we were
the bees' knees, an expression
which delighted them – and me.

Another time they took me up to town,
a special treat, for tea
at the Lady Artists' Club.

They taught us limericks as kids,
of a sort that I recall my parents
may have considered unsuitable.

Their burnside garden specialised
in blue. Delphinium and pulmonaria
had them enraptured. Me too.

They traded plant cuttings
and seedlings: lavender
and tradescantia, ageratum

and salvia transylvanica,
grape hyacinth, wild violet,
and the horticultural challenge

of meconopsis – whose mere mention
had them hyperventilating
with excited, childlike adoration . . .

Easels on the seashore, their
windswept holidays at Appin were
urgently interrupted in emergency

by car trips to Glasgow
to procure that particular range
or shade of paint

without which they could not capture
a precise Argyll watercolour sunset,
an inscape over Duror . . .

That pinky-beige corduroy
tall willowy lady – hard to imagine her
driving an army lorry in the war.

Easier to visualise the shorter, elder sister
stepping it out with long smart brolly
through the Botanic Garden

whence surreptitious sideshoots were
folded away in that innocuous umbrella
and wafted past unwary park-keepers.

Their dogs – Breughel, a favourite,
then Chudleigh, and a long line of brown-eyed
retrievers often named after artists.

In due course my small son,
also of their name,
hugely entertained them.

'Oh, let him go
upstairs,' they'd cry.
'He only wants to see

if the tap in the bathroom
is dripping yet!' It was,
he would seriously announce,

to howls of indulgent laughter.
'Of course it drips.' And in the car,
later, with wide eyes he'd report,

'I think they both sleep
in one big bed – together.'
'Well, it's cold weather,'

I said. 'People of that age
are bound to feel the cold.
They keep each other warm.

'And anyway,' I added,
warming to my point, 'you
sometimes sleep with mum and me . . .'

Such zest they had and empathy;
such zany sharpness,
such delight in little things –

my filmstar dowagers,
last duchesses,
time-honoured friends.

HOW DO I WRITE A POEM?

Often like this.

Act I

I take a long evening walk.
After a time it gets dark
and my body picks up a rhythm
as words and snatches of phrases,
idioms and puns and wordgames
start shooting star-like in my head.

Sometimes I start to get lucky
and pick up coagulations –
patterns, sentences, sequences,
and I play around with these,
like any astronomer. Words
find each other, bombard
one another like atoms
in a lab experiment. Shards
and odd fragments come together
and coalesce. I'd grow crystals
if I were a chemist, or cultures
if I was discovering penicillin.

It is then that I sometimes think:
'Was that the makings
of a poem or three? Is this
to be one of those evenings?'

More often than not, it's not.
So I think no more about it.

Act II

Sometimes, later on at night,
after a bath or some other work,
I sit down with pen and paper
and revisit the mental sequences
that accompanied my walk.

Semi-legibly, often in no kind of order,
I slam them down on the page.
Then I leave them, and go to bed,
and sleep the sleep of the just.

Act III

Later, maybe next morning,
or after some weeks or months,
I may return to my scribbles,
recalling the rhythms and feelings
that accompanied my walk
of last night or of weeks ago.

If they still give a positive charge
(i.e. if I've not forgotten them),
I will then type out my scribbles,
turn the odd cliché through ninety degrees,
filleting as I go. Then begins
to emerge the skeleton of a poem.

Act IV

Act IV is to read the draft
to a group of critical listeners.
They tell me if I'm saying anything
to them. If they start to go on
about the form of the poem,
I know I'm on a hiding to nothing –
the medium has fogged the expression.

Best advice if this happens: bin it.

Act V

Last phase of all:
I sometimes try and get the poem printed
in a book or magazine. Occasionally
I am successful. Usually
I forget who I've sent the damn thing to,
but nowadays I try
to be a little more methodical
in my poetical efforts.

Coda. A Non-Government Health Warning

The time and motion folk
will be horrified to know
that for every poem of mine
to complete this curious course,

twenty fall at the first hurdle.
Two or three progress as far
as the back of a misplaced envelope,
or fall down behind a drawer,
or get shoved into some forgotten place.
One in ten makes it as far as Act IV.

A wriggling sperm has more chance
of being the lucky one
that gets to transform
the waiting ovum
than one of my poems has
to see the light of print.

So what? That
doesn't bother me too much –
nor stop me doing it.

II
CLIMBER'S CALENDAR

SKYE NOCTURNE

We lie on hard ground
under a map of stars
sensing the inky outline of high hills.

Beyond the midnight breeze
a lonely curlew pipes her eerie note
while nearer by the tent flaps lazily.

I turn to you
and pull your sleeping body close,
curling myself around you.

The form, the heft, the warmth
of you, are all I know
or wish to know.

Say nothing to me now
for I am overcome
by this touching proximity.

Or say what impulse you have jogged
in the dry white boneyard of my heart
in this Glen Brittle.

5 October 1998

SLIOCH

Standing alone and proud,
'the hill of the spear'
is a tough climb, you warn.

Soon as I see
the great dark distant mass of it,
I know how right you are.

Two days on,
my legs are stiff
in eloquent confirmation.

In sore complaint
my heavy arms
are tenderly articulate.

But my light head, euphoric still,
trails in the clouds
after that fine day on the hill.

7 November 1998

LOCHEARNHEAD

Winter sunrise over the loch:
hills steam in a thin mist
and a rimy frost sparkles
across an empty car park.

The world is asleep and still,
apart from nearby snaps
of cracking ice on frozen branches,
and the buzz of my shaver

from the car. Driving up earlier
I'd seen snow on Stob Binnean,
'hill of the anvil'. A sense
of white expectancy was on the air.

Today after breakfast
by Balquhidder, I hope
to climb it and the 'big hill'
to the north of it – Ben More.

A welcome prospect beckons:
the rendez-vous then comradeship
of climbing, and a cramponned ascent
to the updrafts of the world.

20 December 1998

INTO ATHOLL

Some future midnight
an old man may study the map
on the kitchen table,
drinking tea, remembering
the day we'd hoped to have a go
at Beinn a' Ghlo. But the cloud – dammit –
came down too low.

We settled for Carn a' Chlamain instead,
'the hill of the buzzard' –
boring but safe, you said.

Will he recall the long walk up Glen Tilt
and back, deer cropping at hillsides
facing the Shieling and Bulaneasie,
us shouting at drizzling clouds
to clear off out of it . . . ?

Will he recall climbing in new boots
up from Clachghlas into the white-out
of an Antarctic symphony where you found
a line of boulders and a broken wall
to guide us blindly to a frigid top . . . ?

Will he recall the dragging weight
of wet kit, wet boots, wet hat
skewed low over chilled ears,
heavy eyebrows drooping with snow . . . ?

All that effort for a tick
on a list of impervious Gaelic names –
hard, timeless and implacable
like the hills they denote.

Or will he remember fish suppers
at Pitlochry, a shared bottle
of lemonade, the sting of heat
returning to wind-lashed faces,
chilblained hands and aching feet . . . ?

23 January 1999

MEALL GHAORDIE

Possibly 'the rounded hill
of the shoulder, arm or hand',
pronounced *myowl girday*.

A quick trot up from Tullich farm
past a scatter of high shielings
to left and right –
deserted, ruined, wind pierced
huddles of stones to remind
of the time when people lived
on the heights of Glen Lochy
and in the forest of Mamlorn.

Then ankle-deep through heather
and deepening snow cover
until the final, silent lap,
slipping and scrambling
over the black boulders
of Castail Samhraidh,
'the summer castle' –
perhaps a shepherd's lookout
in days before the Clearances.

At last a soft, mysterious roar
impinges on the consciousness,
and soon we realise
we are hearing the din of heaven –
the onslaught of an arctic gale
hurled over the summit ridge
that we now approach
from a sunnier, sheltered south.

Our goal a white trig point
shivering within a broch-like cairn
where we shelter from the blast
to survey Glen Lyon
and a distant Moor of Rannoch.

We linger long enough up there
to watch our eyebrows
turn bushy white and comical
with ice, before beating retreat
with neither speech nor ceremony,
and carefully descending
south-facing, glistening, silent slopes.

7 February 1999

EAST OF GLENSHEE

Leggy white hares play and lope
on a midday, sunny, snowy slope
between Meall Gorm and Creag Leacach
('blue hill' and 'slabby crag').

The ridge up to the whited dome
of Glas Maol ('grey-green hill')
has black and white screes to left
and perfect cornices to right of us.

The walk towards Cairn of Claise
('hill of the hollow') gives longer views
to curving Cairngorms (more 'blue hills')
and the dark sentinel of Lochnagar
('little loch of the noisy sound').

The ski tow disgorges distant stick-folk
to glide down and out of view
while we traverse a dozen types of snow,
slushing, sliding, crunching, kicking in.

Turning east for the little cairns of Tolmount
and Tom Buidhe ('hill of the valley'
and 'yellow hill'), there is a glimpse
of Jock's Road down to wooded Glen Doll.

Returning west, the world darkens as
wearily we enter a passing snowstorm
and feel our way with luck and compass
towards Carn an Tuirc ('hill of the boar').

By slow instalments the white-out lifts.
Bits of blue sky and hill reappear
and our final top is not just visible
but resplendent in a winter sunset.

14 March 1999

LOOKING WEST

I dream we are two Viking jarls
today, with simple action plans
and strategies – along the lines
of take life by the throat;
travelling in thrall into high places
spying out these wide Hesperides

from Skye's blue jagged Cuillin
to Jura's rounded paps, Kintyre
and even far-off Arran's hazy peaks
and all the lateral wonders
of a world adjacent and between
the blest islands of the west:
Iona, Colonsay,
Coll and Tiree,
the Uists, Barra, Mingulay,
stretching into the blue,
with Staffa, Ulva, Eorsa nearer to
our vantage point of Mull's big hill.

This summit is among the high points
of two lives. Mind how you go,
you two. Evade descent.
Postpone the parting handclasp.
Consider another golden moment
and reflect. Beyond this pinnacle
a setting sun declines
into the anecdotage of Valhalla
and the sea, for everything
that rises has to ebb.

16 April 1999

MEALL NAN TARMACHAN
'HILL OF THE PTARMIGAN'

Hints of mist and haze
surround a soft spring day.
Almost no wind.

Beyond the summit cairn
a young grouse interrogates us
from a dwindling snowfield.

A large frog quizzes us
from under a lump of peat.
I wonder what frogs do
in a heron-free zone
above three thousand feet.

On the way down
are tadpoles in clear lochans
in writhing black zillions.
Deer on a dun-coloured hill
crop audibly, barely visible.

But not a ptarmigan
in sight all day.

24 April 1999

THE BEN

Ascent is by the tourist route:
a well trod zigzag path
busy with outdoor pilgrims,
many of them oddly attired
for the ritual climb,
and shedding trails of litter.

A fat lady in flip-flop sandals
mops her glowing brow,
as hang-glider folk
await the right moment
to jump into a hushed void
with multi-coloured canvases,
then float and eddy
down and down.

In summit snow around
the highest trig point in the land
sits a gathering of excited souls
in agitated tracksuits
this bank holiday Monday:
We've made it, announces
the bearded man into a mobile phone,
jumping up and down
and bumping into me.

We peer down precipices
into the dizzy chasm,
swig at water-bottles,
eat our sandwiches.

The steep descent
follows rough bouldery slopes
and the long gracious ridge
of a rocky arête, curving down
and up again to 'the big red cairn',
or Carn Mhor Dearg.
Leftward the endless drop
to Coire Leis ('the grey corrie').

This is the Ben's
deserted side – no litter here,
no tourist route, no
body. Only the crack
and ricochet of snow
sheering from vast cornices
and thundering
on black rocks below.

3 May 1999

FINALLY, THE MAMORES

A quarter century ago or more
in 1973 or 74
I was spending a summer
exploring the Glencoe hills
when I gazed idly across
the dark shadow of Loch Leven
from the Hill of the Thunderbolt –
or was it the Aonach Eagach ridge –
towards the vague blue lines
of the then-unvisited Mamores.
I well recall the thought:
'You're next.'

Yesterday and at long last
I finally had the pleasure
of 'doing' six of them
with you. The day
was all I could have hoped
and more, the Bad Step
and the Devil's Ridge
nice euphemisms
and scary reminders
of the Crazy Pinnacles
all those years before.

I'm glad they waited for us.
After all, what's another
quarter century for hills
in three hundred million years
of metamorphosing?

15 May 1999

MEALL CHUAICH
'HILL OF THE QUAICH'

Exactly as forecast:
a lowering muggy day,
hills cloud-screened and blue
withhold their view.

My matching mood
of subdued grizzle
is a surprise –
presaging what?

Nasty weather from the west?
A bout of spleen? Sundry
meteorological mood swings
on which I'm none too keen?

Light drizzle falls all day
and keeps off the midges,
having already kept us off
the better ridges.

So much for flaming June.

13 June 1999

BEINN ACHALADAIR
'HILL OF THE FIELD OF HARD WATER'

Sheerest perversity of summer
to climb up out of broken sun
only to disappear from view
into a cloud-capped hill – guarantee
of mist and rain and zero visibility.

Outlines of watching sheep and deer
silently pause to downward peer
patiently through swirls of mist
at the panting disturbance
from below: very Landseer.

Feeling our way, we sense
we've reached the summit ridge
when the climbing levels off
and a wet, slapping wind gets up.

Lining up map and compass
in a sudden blatter of rain,
we pick our route along
Achaladair's three ghostly tops.

3 July 1999

INACCESSIBLE PINNACLE

You're doing fine, okay?
Just don't look down.
There's lots of handholds. You don't say!
Where do I put my feet, pray?

There's no going back
beyond this point. I see.
Or do I? No, I must be mad.
I hang on for grim death and pray.

Calmer after a minute
or two, I'm inching upwards
again, trying to ignore
a panic spasm of leg cramp.

Trying too to ignore the plainest fact:
that at least half the holds
on this famous rock are loose, polished
by clammy sweats off climbers' hands.

Abseiling off into the void
is easy, after the 'moderate difficulty'
of that undignified, shaking scramble
up the dizzying east ridge.

2 August 1999

STUC A' CHROIN
'PEAK OF DANGER'

I sit on my second summit
savouring the moment
and looking back at Ben Vorlich.

In space and sunshine
and glittery silence, I watch
tiny figures on the distant ridge.

An old man joins me, nimble
but gnome-like, puffing and panting
after the bouldery scramble.

'Why do we do it?' he asks
with a kingfisher glint
of roguish blue eyes.

'Because we need space
to work it all out,' he adds,
'once in a while – that's why.'

He nods. 'It sorts our heads out
for another week. It helps us
face Monday mornings, doesn't it?

'And we like an adrenaline shot
got from the whiff of danger
picking our way up that buttress.'

As explanations go, I concur
these are about as good
as any I've heard so far.

8 August 1999

LADHAR BEINN
'CLOVEN-SHAPED HILL'

Views from this confluence of ridges
westward to Skye and the small isles
stun in the afternoon haze.
They surpass superlatives.

Proud vanguard of all the mountains
to the north stands Beinn Sgritheall
('hill of the screes'): mirrored steel
blue-grey on a polished loch.

Our first two hills today
were Luinne Beinn and Meall Buidhe
('hill of mirth, or anger' and 'yellow hill'),
foregrounding the east and south
with longer views – serried ranks
from Sgurr na Ciche ('hill of the breast')
rippling back to distant Ben Nevis.

Far below and all around
stretch the rough bounds
of Knoydart: empty ground,
a wilderness we've trekked across
and slept on this weekend.

We pass ruined shielings, and marks
of runrigs through the ferns
where vegetables once grew.

A sometime home, the bothy
shelters mice and hikers now –
the people who lived here long ago
transported to the far-off corners
of a baffling world.

Scatter our ashes here
when our time comes,
in the shadow of Ladhar Bheinn
overlooking the loch of heaven.
Return some human traces
into this emptiness.

12 September 1999

BEN CHONZIE
OR BEN-Y-HONE

Honking at one another
a skein of greylag geese flies high
above Loch Turret, breaking
a new day's silence. A heron flaps
nearer the surface of the loch,
calling out hoarsely.
It takes me time to locate
far less identify these sounds
in the vast stillness of the hills.

I walk from the Hill of Weeping
down to Carn Chois, the peaty tops
alive with fat hares, the red grouse
calling, 'Go back, go back!'
and the ptarmigan scuttling away
on white-feathered snowshoes.
Two eagles soar with the thermals
above the glen, checking
for a little light lunch.

I pick a careful, solo path
across the boggy bits
of hill, trying to look ahead
to walks without you.

I shake my head and look away:
the prospect is dizzying,
it is so blank and bare.

Heaped-up snow is in the air.
The silence is all-enveloping
here on the moss today.

5 October 1999

III
PORTFOLIO THREE

TIME'S TRAVERSE

And did I steal a march today
on marching time, when accidentally
at some point of a snowy walk I crossed
an earlier life's path? It brought
an icy blast and crusts of frozen rime,
damp snowflakes from a hoary past
dogging these older footprints
now revisiting the scenes
of some forgotten, youthful crime.

The house, the door came back to me,
the number three,
a leafy square across the road.
But who it was I'd come to see
remains a mystery —
frustratingly.

Nevern Square, London. March 1998

BARBER-SHOP BLUES

Mainly it's a pleasant trip
every eight weeks or so
to the friendly local barber-shop
where I doze off to the quiet snip, snip
of Barber Bill or Barber Joe
and the desultory barber talk.

A thing I detest is the sight
of those shorn locks of purest white
sitting in my lap, a snowdrift bright.

My hair's nut brown, I want to say –
or it was brown the other day,
so why can't it just stay that way?

I disown it, please take it away.
That evidence that I am human clay
is inadmissible, I want to say.

BIRTHDAY LARGESSE

For some years
it was her custom
and her pleasure
to distribute birthday largesse
in cash form – £1 notes
for each year of our lives:
our family's version
of the Royal Maundy.

Before her death
I had arrived
at the munificence of £55
slipped inside my birthday card.

Aged about ten, one of her grandsons,
saving up to buy himself a bicycle,
announced a fervent desire
to be a hundred.

MEDAL

I have the photo still:
myself aged four, podgier
and more curly haired
than I have since become.

Dad stands behind
smart in dark uniform,
hands resting on my shoulders
for reassurance.

We're flanked by my mother
in checked tweed suit
and my grandmother in pleated dress.
Both wear hats: it's an occasion.

In front of palace gates and railings,
centrepiece to the ensemble,
I hold the medal in its open case,
blue and white silk, a silver cross.

I remember no crowds
but a drab grey morning
luminous with excitement.
We were going to see the King.

I was hot and fidgetting
through the long ceremony,
but a tall guardsman lifted me
onto a high radiator for a better view.

There was a long queue
of men shaking the King's hand,
talking to him, receiving their awards.
This was their big day.

'What did he say?'
'He asked me what I got it for.'
'What did you say?'
'For doing my duty, sir.'

★

He kept it many a year.
Then it was gone, stolen
by a door-to-door type
who preyed on the elderly gullible.

I have the black case still,
with empty, cross-indented velvet,
from Garrard's, Goldsmiths,
Jewellers, &c to the King.

BRASS FIGURE

To my nephew Paul Cripps, on his marriage

Before 1930, your grandad (my dad)
brought it home from Calabar
to his mother in Glasgow.

For nearly fifty years
it sat among the clutter
of her kitchen mantelpiece.

After her death it came
and took up shelf-space
on my upstairs landing.

Beside the big brass tray
it stood for over twenty years
keeping a quiet eye on us.

I loved its rounded beard,
its strange two-pointed headdress,
its ceremonial hunting horn.

I loved the shiny patina
of its surfaces, the criss-cross
patterns of its kilt and hat.

I imagined it
more tribal priest than king,
our soothsayer in residence.

Something tells me
now's a good time for it to be
your little household god.

Consult it from time to time
if just to dust it once a year —
it's ready for another hearth.

I trust you'll find it grows
into a friendly presence,
a benign familiar.

KITCHEN CLOCK

I used to wind it for her.
'Once a week, thirty turns
of that old metal key that sits
on top of it,' she'd said. 'And
every Sunday, mind. One day
it will sit in your kitchen,'
she'd added with a not-sad look
that said, 'Before too long.'

We painted it red when it came to us
and sat it over the kitchen fireplace.
True to custom, every Sunday morning
I stand on a chair, and reaching up
I wind it still. In a week it gains
about ten minutes, so on Sundays
I also knock the big hand back
after checking the 'right' time
on one of the digital contraptions –
all of them slightly at variance.

Nowadays I realise
that this old clock is going
to outlive me too. Sometimes
I wonder idly to whom
will fall the ritual
of the Sunday wind-up.

Today I stand on the kitchen chair
and listen to it once again
for a minute or two.
'Clocks don't keep time –
they just keep up with it,'
sounds like its steady refrain.

SCHOOL REUNION

or, Thirtysomething years on

It can't be Aggie Thom — but yes!
And is that person, can it really be
Macpherson E?
It is, it is.
And look —
there's David Agassiz.

Who'll be the next?
And can I tell
if I will recognise him?
Here's Carswell,
not Stewie, no, but R S L. And yes,
in spite of all the years,
and all the silly private fears
of shyness and I don't know what,
I know them instantly:
changed, and yet not changed,
quite uncannily.

One good if gangly runner of middle distances,
one petty officer, dapperish and neat,
one focussed moth collector, all engrossed,
one scrummager and house anchor-man —
I recall all this. Have they been
through my life with me?
Where have I filed away
these brothers of my youth,
who have trouble recollecting
my yesterdays today?

Where are the youths of yesteryear?
Back they all come in floods of memory.
Where Dougie Craib or Bellybeer?
What of young Blair,
who used to like
to comb his well combed hair?
Is it still there? Is he?
I think of x and y and zee,
brief comrades of a year or three.

And afterwards:
is it not passing strange that I
can pick these people out
with blinding clarity
under the footlights of my brain
as if I'd seen them last
no more than a
companionable week ago?

We come back to school maybe
in later life, like this, as to our own
clear upland stream from some dark, silty sea –
eel-like, or as the salmon, seeking
our flickering beginnings. Do we
not congregate to take an evening
out of the buffeting twilight
of our lives – sociably taking stock
from our collective pasts –
to help us hurtle on towards the night,
shooting the remaining rapids
and tumults into our roaring futures?

TO MY SON, ANDREW

On going to work in Australia

There is no formula I can give you,
other than these few jottings
culled from the travelling days
of my own so-distant youth.

Live in harmony with yourself,
and next to your conscience
look to your health – for these
are blessings money doesn't buy.

Take life one day at a time
and do not plan ahead too far.
Strive for balance – rest after toil,
and steer a middle course.

Stay focused, keeping a sense
of direction. Remember where
you're going, and that
you're still finding yourself.

Know that the journey may be long
and everyone makes his own itinerary.
Don't stray too far from yours,
nor let others presume to impose.

Bully no one, let no one bully you.
Keep a cheerful countenance
and feast your eyes and ears,
pondering all you see and hear.

Be true to yourself,
have pride in yourself,
allow some time for solitude
and contemplation.

Platitudes aside, I contemplate
our short drive to the airport
with your mother, this late summer
afternoon, thinking how little time ago

it was since first we drove you home
that spring day from the hospital –
daffodils everywhere to welcome you
after a hasty birth.

'You can call that one Speedy,'
the midwife had said admiringly
as she nipped out of the birthing suite
for a quick cigarette.

Bon voyage, son, come back soon
and tell us all about Pacific sunrises,
Barrier Reefs, antipodean sunsets
and other travellers' tales.

7 September 1999

SONNET FOR MY WIFE

Another year: can they not go
a little slower? Now I know
how fast we wither into truth,
how far we travel from our youth.

Twenty-one summers are not long
to listen to your special song.
To love your even, smiling ways
a hundred summers were too brief a phase.

We gathered rosebuds long ago
before the winters came, or snow.
So let us gather rosebuds now
to deck your wifely brow.

Shine on your stem, my timeless rose,
through half my life my Frances grows.

21 September 1995

FAREWELL TO SAINT-MALO

You, there, on the end of a receding pier
waving – not drowning – as you disappear
from view. I, on the ferry, way out here
pause to wipe away the inevitable tear
as I wave farewell to you, my dear,
and to *nos belles vacances*
en douce France.

LA BAUDUNAIS

For Jean-Baptiste Robert, died 15 April 2000

This hamlet was your corner of the world.
You shared it with us, told us how it was
when the blossoms of a thousand apple trees unfurled
their piquant fragrance on a country nose.

You quoted Ronsard, trained to comfort souls,
then took a wife, went back to farm the land;
you kept a dog, raised rabbits and a laugh,
you ploughed your furrow, took your neighbour's hand.

Before tap water and electric light
you raised a family here, you dug a well;
you donned a uniform, went off to fight,
but you were lucky – you returned from hell.

You walked at evening out across the fields,
you cycled to the village for your bread,
an old French peasant with a flat cloth cap
to keep the sun or rain from off your head.

Your face would light up with remembered jokes
that made you laugh until you almost cried.
Thus was it from the first day that we met
until the afternoon before you died.

The apple trees are almost gone
and the children have all grown –
and flown. The world is not the same
without them, it is true.

It is different again, dear neighbour,
without you.

BY THE RIVER AT LANGON

Today we walk by the river,
taking the afternoon sun.
Yellow it shines on the oilseed rape
and warms the strollers, every one.

The fishermen sit by the river
trying for an eel or a fish.
'We'll bring some back for supper,' they sigh.
Their wives shrug, 'Oh yes, I wish.'

The trains shoot over the river
taking passengers into the towns.
We wave to the folk at the windows.
They stare back at us with dark frowns.

The Langon charollais coo
wants her poo
and lifts her tail
in a gust of spring hail.
Her udder judders
each time she shudders,
she picks her toof
with a muddy hoof.
Boo-hoo says the Langon coo . . .

Tonight I listen to the midnight showers
as Monsieur Hibou hoots to his perching mate.
The kitchen clock chimes through the wee small hours.
The wind in the sighing trees is desolate.

Strange images shunt across the inward eye
through the long watches of a sleepless night.
Then songbirds start their twitter in the sky
and jolt me out of darkness towards daylight.

BIRDWATCHING

Strutting their hen-toed stuff across the grass,
headbutting one another for bits of broken bread,
I watch a bunch of cackling, birdbrained rooks.
Who rules this roost? Who's cock of this walk?
Who turns chicken? Ah me, stone the crows –
is that a bird of a different colour? I digress.

The Roman augur used to watch the birds,
his job to work out what their conduct meant
in terms of civic auspices; hence to forecast
the wisdom – or not – of public enterprises
projected and to come.

What would the augur make of rooks, I wonder –
a bunch of feathered thugs and headbangers?
What is it like to have a hard and pointy nose,
packing a nasty-looking lethal punch?
Prognosco ergo sum, King Crow seems to say,
and then with raucous caw he feints away.

Spring 1996

SUBURBAN FOXES

One misty evening from a bush of ghosts
suddenly from dewy gorse glided the fox.
He stood there staring at me, I at him,
unmoving, frozen on the fuzzy air.

Again last night, slinking across
a moonlit road outside the hospital
a mangy, scrawny one, too thin for health,
flitted past the sign that says 'Out Patients'.

Another sighting: once after heavy rains
had pelted human life indoors, I ventured out
through weather window to enjoy a watery sun
and saw two of them play in a sodden field.

Soundlessly racing by a burn in spate,
wheeling about in mute and silent romp,
drying off glowing fiery coats,
revelling while it lasted in rain's default.

Today a coupling pair of them
are rapt in a noiseless consummation,
their lives depending on a dance
of ravishment and dedication.

Gaping, I stand transfixed beside a tree,
not wishing to disturb the moment. They
carry on with their lives regardless, but
let me know they know that I am there.

Exiting left, I tiptoe off, grasping my news
of a wooded screen at the foot
of a slope of well-kept gardens that
a new generation of foxes will soon be calling home.

Emerging into the road from this shade of green,
still marvelling at all I've seen,
I wait as heavy traffic thunders by
not twenty yards from a foxes' sanctuary.

Spring 1996

IN THE NAME

Mark this face: black beard,
black eyes, black hatred.
It appears to be the face of evil,
of madness, of religion.

First he fills the morning air
with heat-seeking nouns
and adjectives.
Then the bombs come.

'Not our fault,' he says,
'but God's will.' Then,
piously, he walks away
to make his next pronouncement.

This man would not connect,
he would destroy.
This man has cash.
This man has followers.

He has a bloody nerve.
His hands are bloodier.

September 2001

DIAGNOSIS

I was well up in years
before I understood
that being in love
was a bit like sporting
a serious heart condition.

The doctors called it
paroxysmal atrial fibrillation
and shook their heads,
bless them. Eventually, I accepted
that I was in love.

Did I feel dizziness, sickness,
or lightheadedness,
they asked.
All of the above,
I said. Besides, great joy.

A warning ploy
to lovers, perhaps: no pain,
no gain? Or as my forebears
dourly did once maintain:
ye'll pay for it?

IF . . .

If people brought
to the art of living
a tenth of the zest you bring
to the eating of a beetroot,
the climbing of a hill,
or the parking (or polishing) of a car . . .

If they could focus
with your gusto
on ironing a shirt or riding a bike . . .
Or if they could cram anything
as precarious as a brief weekend
with such limitless horizons . . .

they'd be making tyre tracks
towards a sensational existence
or they'd be flat on their backs
pushing up little blue forget-me-nots.

THE BIG SHEPHERD OF ETIVE
'BUACHAILLE ETIVE MOR'

One long-ago midsummer's day
in tee-shirt and shorts I lingered
on Stob Dubh to watch the sun's
leisurely decline towards Mull, a world waiting.

Last Sunday: a dreich January day,
low cloud and hail, a howling gale,
a chilly dash more suited to wintrier years
offering few views in any direction.
Youth or age, long views or none?

Nice to see the Big Shepherd's ridge
so unchanged, expansive as ever,
even if my own mutations of thirty years
now pit a slowing body-clock
and dimming head-torch
against dark's onset.

WALKING THE MONADHLIATH

You've said how boring these hills are,
but I am not put off. I've never yet
had a boring walk in your company
and today is as exceptional
as any other.

In splendid if mysterious isolation
sitting athwart the long walk-in
is a tin-can stalkers' hillside bothy
(or a halfway house of trolls?)
to impel a wintry war-dance.

Towards the first white summit
mountain hares scatter uphill –
waves of mercury defying gravity:
all silvery, with long-legged suspension
making for deep cover.

We follow lines of fence-posts
through drifts of uneven snow.
Now and then the ghost of a sun breaks
gold and creamy through the white-out,
helping us pick out bearings right and left.
Are these Elysian fields?

Coming off the last summit,
a scrambled race against the winter dark,
we squelch through an icy bog
under the kind of starry sky
only to be seen in country places.

Impossible not to marvel then,
tired, cold and hungry as we are –
what tiny bundles of dreams are men,
how minuscule our own birling Earth-star
within an infinite galaxy.

26 November 2000

YOU AND ME

A modern waulking – walking? – song, for Steven

Low tide at Lochcarron
observing the herons:
you and me
from a tent among birch trees.

The songbirds of morning
are making sweet music:
you and me waking
in the campsite at Morvich.

The sunrise is glancing
off Shenavall bothy:
you and me checking
if anyone's home.

On the vast beach at Sandwood
watching tides thunder:
you and me jumping
on a rock in the bay.

Wet cloud on Black Cuillin,
roping up for an abseil:
we swing down the chimney
in the lap of the gods.

The garrons of Loch Pattack
trot up and inspect us:
us more engrossed
by a lizard on Carn Dearg.

Cycling at twilight
down the track from Ben Alder:
us sniffing then braving
the deer in their hundreds.

Eight low-flying swans,
white V on brown bracken:
us climbing above them
one autumn in Rannoch.

Stags rut in Strathfarrar,
snow smatters the summits:
you and me tasting
a first winter walk.

From the auld brig at Garva
we watch the black river:
you and me throwing
ice blocks in the Spey.

Coming off Beinn Fhionnlaidh
one sharp winter sunset:
you and me after
a day on the hills.

TINSELTOWN, USA

With apologies to Denis Stewart

Like the man said
at the gas-station,
not more 'n ten percent
of the folk
in this goddam town
are real.

SIC TRANSIT

Sound
  fades
    recedes
      and dies away

Silence
  grows
    pervades
      endures

ONE LINERS: A PUNNET

Sit by an early-morning pond and ponder

Poem with a message: a loaded ode

Nature avoids a void

NOTES

AYRSHIRE RECESSIONAL
Sequence of poetry written after my mother's death (December 1996). In addition to feelings of bereavement it grapples with my realisation of the loss of my geographical roots, my mother being the last family link with the place where I grew up. [page 3]

HARPERCROFT
A farm on Dundonald Hill. As a youngster, I figured that it took its name from lands feued to the medieval harpers whose job was to entertain the nearby court at Dundonald Castle. [page 3]

THE BARNS O AYR BURN WEEL
Reference to an episode recorded by Blind Harry, Sir Walter Scott and others. Tradition had it that William Wallace saw the distant fire from the vantage point of Barnweil – named, according to some, because of the Patriot's reputed comment that the Barns of Ayr (with English soldiers imprisoned inside) burned well. The nineteenth-century tower is a Victorian monument commemorating this story from the Scots wars of independence. [page 6]

SWAN LAKE
Ornamental stretch of water in the gardens of Culzean Castle, near Maybole, a haven for birdlife and a favourite place for walking. [page 7]

SKEAGH-BUSH
Fairy bush (from Irish Gaelic). In rural Ireland, thorn trees, wells and raths (mounds) often have supernatural associations with the wee folk. [page 14]

FRONT ROOM and the READING ROOM
References to Trinity College Dublin, where I was a student in 1963. Old Bartkus was my landlord, and he occasionally bought me a pint, especially after a successful day at the Leopardstown racecourse. [pages 17–18]

ST LEONARDS
Inner-city area of Edinburgh facing the spectacular cliffscape of Salisbury Crags and Arthur's Seat. Completion of this recitation piece in 1992 was provoked by news that part of Edinburgh's civic millennial effort was to be the construction of a dinosaur museum at the foot of the Crags (now the Dynamic Earth visitor centre). [page 34]

LANGON, BESLÉ, SAINT-JUST
Villages in the Pays de Redon, in the southern part of Brittany. [pages 50–55; 105]

COTE SAUVAGE
The coast between Piriac-sur-Mer and Le Croisic in south Brittany, parts of which are very rocky. [page 58]

GLEN BRITTLE
The main access point for climbing the Black Cuillin hills of Skye, whence several footpaths give access to the main ridge. There is a campsite by the shore, at the road-end. [page 69]

LA BAUDUNAIS
Hamlet near the village of Renac, about 10 km north of Redon, in Brittany. [page 104]

ACKNOWLEDGEMENTS

Thanks are due to editors of newspapers, periodicals and anthologies in which versions of some of this poetry has already appeared: *The Herald, Poetry Scotland, InScotland, Markings, Fife Lines, West Coast Magazine, Northwords, Lines Review, Poetry Today, Ulster Graduate, OF Newsletter, A Nest of Singing Birds* (1995), the John Muir Trust *Journal & News*, and *The Scottish Mountaineering Club Journal*. Six poems were first published in a School of Poets leaflet (entitled *Retrospective*, 1998). The author acknowledges encouragement and constructive criticism over several years from fellow members of the School of Poets in Edinburgh.

The first section of this book, *Ayrshire recessional and other poems*, was published by Harpercroft in 1998; the second section, *Climber's calendar*, appeared in pamphlet form from the same imprint in 2001. Some poems in these collections have been revised slightly for this book.